My State
KENTUCKY

By Christina Earley

TABLE OF CONTENTS

A Crabtree Seedlings Book

Crabtree Publishing
crabtreebooks.com

School-to-Home Support for Caregivers and Teachers

This book helps children grow by letting them practice reading. Here are a few guiding questions to help the reader build his or her comprehension skills. Possible answers appear in red.

Before Reading:

- What do I know about Kentucky?
  - *I know that Kentucky is a state.*
  - *I know that Kentucky has a horse race called the Kentucky Derby.*

- What do I want to learn about Kentucky?
  - *I want to learn which famous people were born in Kentucky.*
  - *I want to learn what the state flag looks like.*

During Reading:

- What have I learned so far?
  - *I have learned that Frankfort is the state capital of Kentucky.*
  - *I have learned that Mammoth Cave is the largest cave system in the world.*

- I wonder why...
  - *I wonder why the state flower is the goldenrod.*
  - *I wonder why there are vaults of gold at Fort Knox.*

After Reading:

- What did I learn about Kentucky?
  - *I have learned that it is possible to see a moonbow at Cumberland Falls.*
  - *I have learned that the state animal is the Eastern gray squirrel.*

- Read the book again and look for the glossary words.
  - *I see the word **capital** on page 6, and the word **moonbow** on page 21. The other glossary words are found on pages 22 and 23.*

KENTUCKY

I live in Louisville. It is on the Ohio River.

The Louisville Slugger Museum and **Factory** is in my city.

Kentucky is in the southeastern United States. The **capital** is Frankfort.

Fun Fact: Louisville is the largest city in Kentucky.

The state animal is the Eastern gray squirrel.

The goldenrod is the state flower.

We grow a lot of corn in Kentucky. Some of it is used to make popcorn.

Fun Fact: Kentucky **produces** about 274 million bushels of corn a year.

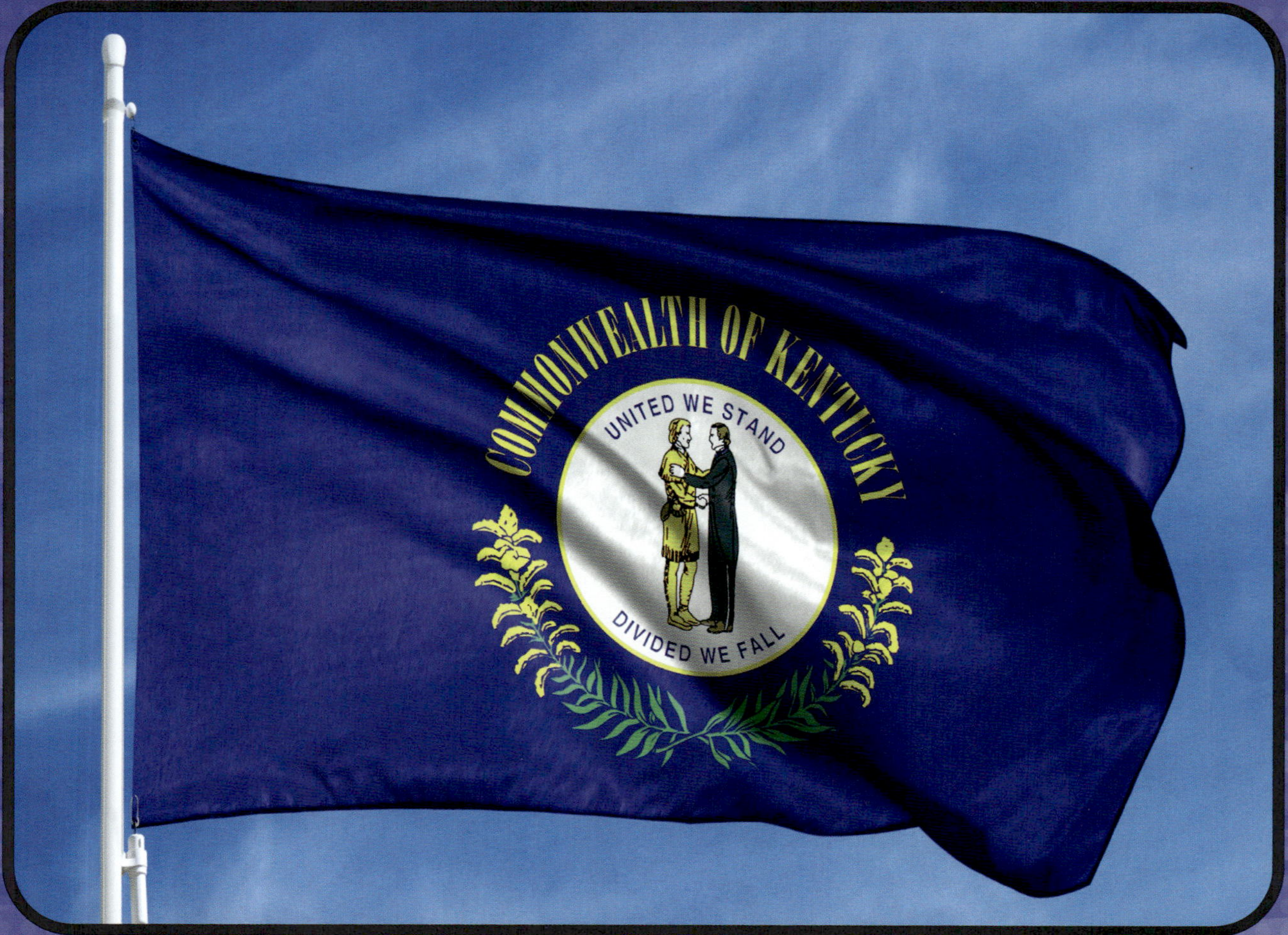

My state flag is blue. The state **seal** is in the middle.

The Kentucky Derby horse race is held every year in Louisville.

I like to explore Mammoth Cave. Sometimes I see bats!

Fun Fact: Mammoth Cave is the longest cave system in the world.

I like to go biking in Daniel Boone National Forest.

There are **vaults** with gold in them at Fort Knox.

Actress Jennifer Lawrence was born in Kentucky. Boxer Muhammad Ali was also born in Kentucky.

Fun Fact: President Abraham Lincoln was born in Hodgenville, Kentucky.

I love hiking in Cumberland Gap National Historical Park.

I can see a beautiful **moonbow** at Cumberland Falls.

Glossary

capital (cap-ih-tuhl): The city or town where the government of a country, state, or province is located

factory (fak-tor-ee): A building where machines are used to make things

moonbow (moon-boh): A rainbow made by moonlight

produces (pruh-doos-es): Makes or grows something for sale or use

seal (seel): A special design that is used on important papers and other items

vault (vawlt): A large, locked room, usually underground, that is used for keeping things safe

Index

About the Author

Christina Earley lives in sunny South Florida with her husband and son. She enjoys traveling around the United States and learning about different historical places. Her hobbies include hiking, yoga, and baking.

Written by: Christina Earley
Designed and Illustrated by: Bobbie Houser
Series Development: James Earley
Proofreader: Melissa Boyce
Educational Consultant: Marie Lemke M.Ed.

Photographs:
Alamy: The Photo Access/Steven Bullock: p. 13
Shutterstock: Alexey Stiop: cover; anthony heflin: p. 3; Sean Pavone: p. 4; Hendrickson Photography: p. 5, 22; Volina: p. 6, 22; Brian E Kushner: p. 8; Apostle: p. 9; Serg64: p. 10-11; Fotokostic: p. 11, 23; Millenius: p. 12, 23; Ko Zatu: p. 14-15; Zack Frank: p. 15; Jim Vallee: p. 16; Phonlamai Photo: p. 17, 23; lev radin: p. 18 left; Featureflash Photo Agency: p. 18 right; Everett Collection: p. 19; Zack Frank: p. 20; Jim Vallee: p. 21, 22

Crabtree Publishing

crabtreebooks.com 800-387-7650

Printed in the U.S.A./072023/CG20230214

Published in Canada
Crabtree Publishing
616 Welland Avenue
St. Catharines, Ontario
L2M 5V6

Published in the United States
Crabtree Publishing
347 Fifth Avenue
Suite 1402-145
New York, New York, 10016

Library and Archives Canada Cataloguing in Publication
Available at Library and Archives Canada

Library of Congress Cataloging-in-Publication Data
Available at the Library of Congress

Hardcover: 978-1-0398-0516-3
Paperback: 978-1-0398-0548-4
Ebook (pdf): 978-1-0398-0612-2
Epub: 978-1-0398-0580-4